R

Norena Ventosa

BookLeaf
Publishing
India | USA | UK

Presentation by *BookLeaf Publishing*

Web: www.bookleafpub.com

E-mail: info@bookleafpub.com

ISBN: 9789358310047

First edition 2023

DEDICATION

This book is dedicated to the younger version of me. La que no sabia que era capaz de tener sueños y lograr metas más grandes que ella misma. The shy little girl who flourished to be the brave woman she is today.

"And who knows but that you have come to your royal position for such a time as this?"

- Esther 4:14

Waves

I love the little things in life
I always have
I love the stillness of time, peaceful auras and
breathtaking yet warm, encompassing energy
I love culture and traditions and the differences
in love, language and beliefs all rooted in the
same soil but so widely diverse in their own
beautiful way
I crave feeling and emotion and a similar
passion and appreciation for this one wild yet
precious life
I love observing
I love understanding
And sometimes my silence is misinterpreted by
what may seem like nothingness suspended in
the air when truly I'm in awe
I'm admiring
I'm connecting
I lost myself in this rush to push for more and
more and more and to treat each day like I'm
fighting and searching and swimming
…and when I stopped myself and let the waves
hit I panicked
Only to now realize, I was drowning in shallow
waters

Had I just reminded myself who I was, what I
loved and lived for
I would've realized that I was as powerful as the
waters that surrounded me.

Lost

I cried over the parts of me I had lost
Not knowing that I was shedding old skin
Necessary to make space for new beginnings
It was only recently that I discovered
That I didn't lose myself
I found myself
And once I found myself
I just couldn't abandon me again

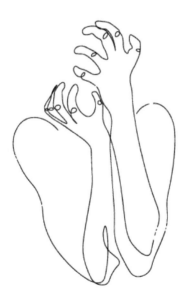

House of Worry

It is strange to grow up in a place decorated with
faith but a faulty story
Doubt, guilt, manipulation, house of worry
Don't you see that what's crumbling is what has
been inside
But you have the nerve to ask me why
Why do I leave to escape the debris
To find clarity
To finally breathe
Without the weight holding me down
To be able to laugh without any guilt
To be able to feel freely
To hear my voice speak loud and clearly
To wake up in a place that allows light to fill the
space within
I'm sorry for the little girl that wasn't able to
escape back then
That thought that all of the weight was hers to
carry
That tried to toughen up so young
Now she's filled with masc energy
A tough external hard shell to protect
The only organ that will allow love, hurt and all
feelings
Necessary to confide and trust
Necessary to feel real

You are worthy
It's like an Angel heard my cries
I want to feel soft again
I want to trust in people, in strangers, in
humanity
I want transparent walls of faith
Where I can trust my intuition and set my
anxiety and darkness free
Where I can give it to God
And let God's timing be
Because I am worthy
I am capable of all things
I am God
God is me
And worry does not live here
In this home, we are free

You used to tell me
Don't climb you'll fall and cry
Don't run you'll fall and cry
Don't cry, you won't fix anything
And now look at me
I'm flying
And if I fall
I'll make my way up again
Even with tears in my eyes
Even if I cry

Greatest Love

She took my breath away
Day and night
Over the highway
Between the train lines
The photos never do her justice
But when you meet her, you feel her greatness
That's all you need
I loved her
But she wasn't mine to keep
The closer I got the farther she stood
Behind the trees
The less I saw her
And God all I wanted to do was see her
Hold her in my hands
Stare into her eyes
I tried to pick her up from the sky
But it casted nothing but darkness
In my pocket, she didn't shine
God whispered,
Something so beautiful
Wouldn't you want to share it with the world
He was painfully right
I crumbled upon setting her back
It killed me inside
But she rose every night
To remind me
That the greatest act of love
Was setting her back into the sky
Where her beauty was shared
Even though her stare lived in my thoughts
And her love was mine

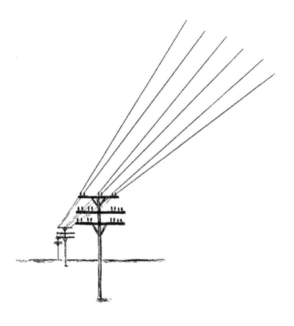

Don't. lose. hope.

A shining star in the dark night sky
The one last sparkle of hope telling you to hold
on when you just want to cry
Because the world seems too big for you and
your dreams sometimes
Can a speckle of dust make a difference and
actually change lives?
The morning silence when you can't get out of
bed
Surrounded by the whispers of "Mija, you can't
give up now" floating in your head
The battle of surrender and fight til your last day
The vanishing floor as you climb up that ladder
often leaving you
Paralyzed, afraid
That shining star in the dark sky
Reminding you to keep going
Even though for now you might not understand
why

Lost

She lost her voice, forgot how to speak freely
Her mind now screams loudly
"Can anyone hear me"
The chaos remains
Everything floats in her head
She can't help but wish
She was someone else instead
She doesn't want to think anymore
Every time she reflects, she is torn
What to do
What to say
What to feel
Who to be
Who to see
When to try
When to fly
When to be
Unapologetically her,
Or mistakenly me

Does it even exist

I want a hopeless romantic type of love
Yes, the love that they sold us in movies
The kind where you always end up exactly
where you're supposed to be
The kind that finds you when you most need it
The kind that holds you and warms your soul
without even trying
The kind that makes you laugh uncontrollably
for hours
The kind that feels peacefully consuming
The 'thinking of you' messages and phone calls
mid day
Shared songs and mixtapes
Long endearing glances
A hand you'll never get tired of holding
A passionately friendly love
Dates full of warm caresses, wet kisses and
gentle hugs

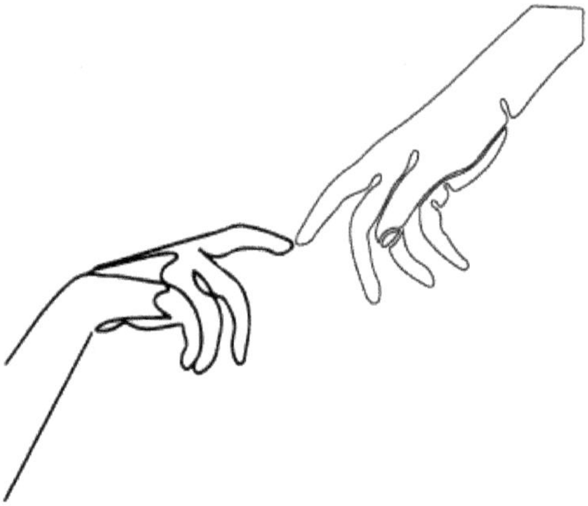

Alive, again

La veces que me pierdo en tu mirada

En esos momentos se siente como he esperado
tanto tiempo para encontrarte

Y al fin te tengo por de frente de mi

Por fin te veo

Por fin te siento

El mundo sigue dando sus vueltas.

Los minutos siguen pasando

Y la vida de otros continúa

Pero el momento contigo se detiene

Y puedo sentir todo lo que estoy

describiendo usando mi cuerpo como un

instrumento

Siento el poder del aire llenando y saliendo de
mis pulmones

Y lo rápido que la sangre me corre por mis
venas

A través de cada centímetro de mí

Alive.

Contigo estoy viva de nuevo

Y mi cuerpo por fin se recuerda
Depues te tanto tiempo

Lo que es estar viva

Su mirada

It was all in her eyes
Had I looked sooner I would've realized
The powerful chills she could send through me
The way she read me with her stare
Her lovely soft, yet bold glare
For weeks I didn't
God, I almost missed it
Felt like we just met, but somehow, she knew
me
What a gift
To be able to give off wholesome vibrations of
peace
and excitement at the same time
Can you believe
It was all in her eyes
What I needed, when I needed it
When I least expected it
And now, I'm lost in it
Lost in her eyes
And if she allows it
I'll never look away

Just be

Sometimes,
The less you control
The more you let it flow
They call it trust.
Like our greatest days..
The ones left unplanned
The ones we surrender
The ones we release any expectation or
constraint
On where we should be
Or what we should be doing
Our greatest days
Are the ones spent free
Time exists, only as a construct
The purpose of just being
Is all we need
Our greatest days
Are the days where we plan
You'll just be you
I'll just be me
I like to believe
Trusting you
Set me free

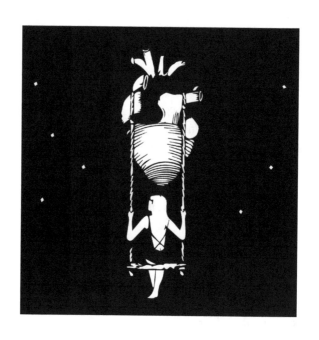

She is the sun

She is the sunrise
Her divine energy leads the new day
Blowing life into the world as the rush of a fresh
start
inspires
productivity and unwanted chaos across
hemispheres
Restless girl
Her rays establish connectivity between a variety
of unfamiliar things, people, and places
Her powerful reach is ignited by her feminine and
masculine fire

She is the sunset
Her kaleidoscope colors are celestial
They are strong-willed and powerful as they fill
the
sky glowing
fearlessly and letting everyone know of her
presence
Her beauty is undeniably one-of-a-kind
Her soul is calming
Her being is loved; unmatched
Screaming "I am me, and I am proud"
In the most elegant way

She is the Sun

She is the moon

She illuminates the night over cities and waters
Whispering calmness after hours of madness
Promising comfort, promising steadiness,
promising peace..
Her perfectly imperfect moon texture
displaying the depth of her story
One that pushes her to be brave and
unapologetically authentic,
Even when she is vulnerable, even when she
feels weak
She sits among the stars, wandering aimlessly in
the dark
as she sheds light on those around her
Filling the night with gentle reminders of what
feels familiar,
what feels like home
when often not receiving anything in return
Humble girl, will she ever learn?
She offers a love so deep and profound causing
an
abundance of ripples and waves
across the ocean leaving everlasting effects on
chosen souls
She quietly glows in every phase, equally
stunning,

despite the parts of her she hides away
Not everyone is deserving of her wholeness, and
she knows it
She may not be the sun,
and honestly she never had the desire to be...
She is not for everyone
She is intricate
She is beautiful
She is wildly unique
She is the moon
She is me

Strawberry Skies

I love everything about you
I whispered
Unconsciously conscious
Letting all my built-up feelings flow
Home where they belong
Without even knowing
I knew what I had said
My mind and body maybe intoxicated
But when the heart speaks
It speaks clearly, uninterrupted
Softly, but strong
When the heart speaks
It's never wrong
Before I even asked
I knew what I had said
All along
Because the thought plays repeatedly
In my head
Like I do
With my favorite songs

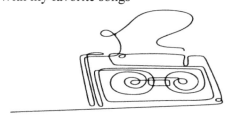

Beach D

The wind pulled us in every direction
You could imagine
Within the shifts and the whirlwind,
We found our peace in a sandstorm of chaos
We stood our ground despite the pressures
around us,
I still saw her and felt her
Without being able to see her and feel her
It is true what they say
Home could feel like much more than just a
place
Home could feel like
A beach chair
A pineapple cooler
A secret beach
Cereal ice cream
A fluffy bed
BLTs
Last but not least,
And in the middle of it all
You and me

Como la luna

Las manchas de nacimiento que viven en tu piel
me recuerdan de las estrellas

Tiene sentido como tu puede brillar sin luz

Aveces me pierdo en tus ojos y no quiero que me
encuentren

Y me asombra como el mundo es tu museo, y tú
la obra maestra

Con solo una mirada, me lleva hasta la luna

Nunca esperaba llegar tan lejos, estando tan
cerca de ti

Y no sé como lo haces

Reset

I wish I could rewire my brain
I'd install new levels of
confidence
Remove any doubtful wires
I'd fix whatever makes me worry about the
future
And add circuits of faith
I'd increase the voltage of living in the moment
Add additional internal storage for meaningful
memories
I would turn the knob up, the one that controls
levels of
Positivity
Love
Softness
I'd repair any trauma and press the reset button
for healing
I'd remove and wash away any built-up fear
I'd tie everything tightly together
Sealed with my restored inner peace
A brand new mind
An indestructible me

"You deserve all great things"

Clouds are necessary for rain
Without them we'd be in a constant drought
But it is exhausting chasing sunshine
With a dark cloud following around
And I understand how all things have purpose
And contribute great things
But it is as if I left a storm to enter another one
And I'm fighting
I'm trying to push myself through
Ignoring the darkness even though I love the
rain, the thunder, and lightning
And this dark cloud isn't new
But it wasn't until now that I've turned around
and decided to face the dark cloud of societal
norms and cultural expectations head-on
Because I love the rain, the thunder, and
lightning
But I love the sun, the light, and its energizing
rays
And I just began to realize
That I am deserving of all the great things

Si se pudo

No one told me there were dreams outside of the
hood
For me, Caryl Avenue was all I knew
All I would be
Apartment 3A
Mi feliz pequeño hogar in the lost borough of
lost dreams
If I could turn back time
Perhaps I wouldn't change a thing
Because the fire hydrant summers, bodega runs
and rooftop sunsets
Allowed me to fully live in the moment
With no worry about tomorrow
Even though tomorrow would bring
More than little me ever knew or could ever
imagine

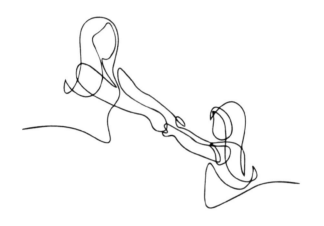

Missing Piece

I can't explain the moment I realized
Exactly what I've felt with and without you
We are a puzzle, you and I
A little part of me
Is literally with you
You hold it close, unknowingly
Somewhere in your warm chest
Somewhere in your deep brown eyes
The moment we're together
It clicks, it fits
The pieces slide into place
Like a lock and key
That has long been misplaced
You fit the space
The space somewhere in my chest
Between my breast
Tilted slightly to the left
The missing piece
It clicks, it fits
My body relaxes
I become free
Free of any tension
My mind blanks
There is nothing worth pondering that is allowed
to take me away

From that wholesome loving 'home at last'
feeling
Of when that piece clicks, fits
Perfectly

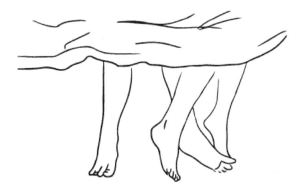

Niña muda

Me preguntaban que si era muda

Que porque no hablaba

No reía

No lloraba

La verdad era

Que no creía que había

Sentido, propósito

Hablar sin poder arreglar

Reír sin poder entender

Como tan fácil olvidarme de lo de ayer

Casita rota y vacía

Lleno de un gran amor de una madre

Orgullosa, valiente y amable

Con raíces extranjero y aveces ignorante

No le hecho la culpa

Ni a ella, ni a nadie

Si me crió como ella supo

Y todo las lecciones

Que me tocaban

Me encontraron tarde o temprano

Y hoy soy

La niña que no hablaba

Pero la mujer valiente y poderosa

Que pudo salir adelante

Confianza

We so easily fear the unknown
Not realizing the magic in the way life unfolds
I'm here to tell you
Loosen the grip, let it flow
There is a plan already in place
I promise you
We can let go
And if it's scary
It's okay
But trust that you had no control in being born
Yet here you are today
Flourishing in what may feel like
Some of your darkest days
Living freely and authentically
Even on your most boring days
La vida es única
entonces, porque nos preocupamos?
Just day by day
You'll find your way
Y luego veras
Que sí, nos encontramos

Printed in the USA
CPSIA information can be obtained
at www.ICGtesting.com
LVHW051836290224
772930LV00020B/1566